TOUGH SKINS

Poems by

P.B. Bremer

TOUGH SKINS

Copyright © 2025 P.B. Bremer

All rights reserved. No part of this publication may be reproduced, distributed, or transmitted in any form or by any means, including photocopying, recording, or other electronic or mechanical methods, without the prior written permission of the publisher, except in the case of brief quotations embodied in critical reviews and certain other noncommercial uses permitted by copyright law. For permission requests, write to the publisher, addressed "Attention: Permissions Coordinator," at the address below.

ISBN: 978-1-959346-88-3 (Paperback)

Library of Congress Control Number: 2025936037

Cover Design (Art): Laura Hahn
Book Design Interior: Robert T Canipe

Printed in the United States of America.

First printing 2025.

Redhawk Publications
The Catawba Valley Community College Press
2550 Hwy 70 SE
Hickory NC 28602
https://redhawkpublications.com

Tough Skins is a tough and dazzling collection of poems. The originality of the language invigorates the reader and keeps us wanting more. Broken into five sections, Bremer's collection takes the reader on an unbridled ride through the streets of derelicts and men struggling to simply live. In other sections, in short and moving lyrics, the poet reflects of life passages. Throughout, the poet's music and language carry us forward. Fearless and original, these poems resonate with an anguished passion that somehow retains a perfect pitch throughout.

—Jonah Bornstein, author of *The Art of Waking, Treatise on Emptiness,* and *Mortar*

P.B. Bremer's *Tough Skins* demonstrates the clear-eyed, cunning intellect of the poet doubling as philosophical gadfly, recalling the work of writers like Alan Dugan, David Ignatow, and Stephen Dobyns. His poems are lean, fearless, and rife with mordant wit and keen music. Flinty observations of human cruelty and frailty are balanced with tremendous empathy for those on the psychological edge, the margins of a gilded America. The imagery is exacting and local, but beckons toward ineffable spaces that are a special province of poetry—the daily appointment with the unknowable, the engagement with looming mortality, the intractable mystery of simply existing—as Bremer writes, "I too must eat from its plate/ scraped clean of meaning,/always the restless guest in its bed.

—Tim Earley, author of *Linthead Stomp, Boondoggle,* and *The Spooking of Mavens*

In *Tough Skins*, P.B. Bremer's debut book of poems, we discover work in the gritty tradition of Charles Bukowski, poems that speak to the depravity of human life, that remember the downtrodden----including the speaker---at their wits' end. Call it Bremer's metaphysic of despair: problematic love, suicides, homelessness, day labor and malt whiskey before tears and climbing three flights in the YMCA to room 302 where he can quit the day and "smoke his last cigarette." But what takes these poems beyond a simple litany of damage is his imagination and striking sense of language, his music (Muddy Waters and Coltrane) and his metaphoric leaps, the "hours that drift/without paddles," "memory's forgotten backcountry," "the silent movie of sleep." These poems feel elegiac and clear-eyed. Meant to be read over again, these poems find salvation in the moment of each word, the poet speaking from "empty moon rooms/of his heart."

—James McKean, author of *Headlong, Tree of Heaven,* and *We Are the Bus*

The Five Remembrances

I am subject to aging. There is no way to avoid aging.

I am subject to ill health. There is no way to avoid illness.

I am going to die. There is no way to avoid death.

Everyone and everything that I love will change, and I will be separated from them.

My only true possessions are my actions, and I cannot avoid their consequences.

—Siddhartha Gautama, the Buddha

For my brother, David Dusing Hibbs (1977-2024)

For all the suicides

CONTENTS

Blackbirds

Night	15
Monday Morning	16
The Thief of Sleep	17
Rabbit Hole	18
Pig	19
Whack Jobs	20
Underbelly	21
Oblivion	22
Pornographia	23
Cold Turkey	24
Blackbirds	25
Calendars	27

The Bumble House

The Bumble House	31
Stranded	32
Three Stains of Winter	33

Memoir   35
Muddy Waters   36
Blue Note   37
Self-Pity   38
Circus   39
Lonely Ones   40
Deep Water   41

Separate Corners

The Basement of Unfinished Sentences   45
Conjunctions   46
Marriage   47
Reconciliation   48
Tattoos   49
Between Sheets   50
8mm Man   51
The Final Bite   52

Tough Skins

Behind These Bars   55

Even Now	56
January 8, 1965	58
Recollections of Mother	59
Toughskins	60
After Recess	61
Mac	63
Hostile Territory	64
Sister Suzie's Head Got Sick One Day	66
Backcountry	67
The Boy in the Box	68
Blue Billy	69
Juvenile Detention, Marion 1981	71
YMCA	72
Vitriol	73
July 1986	74

Calling the Body Home

Opening Act	79
Dead Man Walking	80
Thistle	82
Empty Wallet	83

Two Men Pissing	84
After the Prostatectomy	85
Nausea	86
After Sixty	87
Cremated Remains	88
Eulogy	89
No Quarter	91
Here the Furnace, Here the Fire	92
The Moment Knows	93
Dead Ringer	95
The Branch	96
Forest Prayers	99
Calling the Body Home	100
Acknowledgments	101
About the Author	103

Blackbirds

Night

I too must eat from its plate

scraped clean of meaning,

always the restless guest in its bed.

P.B. Bremer

Monday Morning

Stripped,
fetal

in Monday's
black bed,

terror sows
its suicides,

picks at them
their eyes —

those scabs
that pock

these

their morning's
sour hours.

The Thief of Sleep

That scavenger

that steals

between the pages of stories

that restless men write

from lonely rooms

in friendless towns— Sleepless.

They feed from her plate of nails

the old regrets, failures

stacked like wrecked Cadillacs

burning on the freeway

leading nowhere

out of the graveyard of the heart.

P.B. Bremer

Rabbit Hole

That lonely hotel painted gray,
standing room only, that place
where no love rents a room

where the cook has boiled
his cabbage cold,
each perseveration soiled in salt

and the house band plays on, plays on
despair's dull and senseless note.

Pig

His mind dragged itself across the floor
of its moonless room
where the calcium fragments of stars
went blind with silence
as the dull and airless days
of June unwound themselves—
a funeral dirge of sleepless streets.
The sour gut of reason unraveled,
and the days buried their shabby caskets
in a pharmacy of awful thoughts
which whispered prayers
to the suicide's pistol, to bruised youth,
to the guardian's grave that had no answer.

P.B. Bremer

Whack Jobs

Bring me my brother
every misfit and freak
every fucked-up junkie
needing fixed.
Bob in the back
bought twelve priceless typewriters
with his dead mother's money
and Frank
40 pairs of Crocs
with his wife's college cash.
Gary got so mad
at the cop in his noggin'
he shattered a beer
with a mirror,
jumped Frontier
from Boise to Brooklyn
then rode the bus home
bouncing checks.
Send in the priest, the sheriff
the shrink with her ink blot.
We'll sign our confessions
with a lie's perfect cursive
before hanging ourselves
in the shower with our socks.

Underbelly

Between 13th and Colfax
the crack heads, the pipe whores
squat in the emaciated shade
of anemic trees
bordering Gomorrah's
abandoned and desiccated lot.
They gather shamelessly
to burn their fingers, their lips, their tongues
on oblivion's heart attack
of blackened glass. Downtown
under June sun's
slow rotation of jobless hours
the drunks, the mad, the homeless
pass out on the library lawn
or piss themselves in carousels.
These—the underbelly,
innovation's dead peasants.
They drag garbage carts, dumpster
to dumpster, ramp to ramp,
zero's tale of once and once was
once upon a time
lost in the vapor trail
of their incessant and impotent protest,
collared dogs wheezing at their feet.

P.B. Bremer

Oblivion

Dilaudid's
boil in the blood

its k-bar blade
in the vein

the bomb's blow
the head's nod
the heart's stop

twice kissed—
fucked, forgotten.

Pornographia

Flesh hungers, mind shops
Mind hungers, flesh follows

takes sticky chairs together
in the Pleasure Palace,

her dark heart. *Eat*
she says,
all my pretty pictures

And they do, they do

P.B. Bremer

Cold Turkey

A poisoned blood

of jelly bean pills

drains my veins, mind

tapped and threaded,

teary-eyed, its music

a language I can't understand

as a tide rise of screams

sinks the street

on its bar of summer sun

heating the trees,

brain baking, corpse skin

an itch without a fix.

Blackbirds

Twelve wet heads

sweat on a row of folding chairs,

a dozen blackbirds

dressed in green cotton pajamas

and blue paper booties—

cracked pipes, bent spoons, busted bottles

broken open inside out.

They suck from Dixie cups

their queasy comforts, drag

from packs of Newports

a fog of thoughts.

Dezzy, the fat girl

with Duncan stitched across her tit,

lost her teeth

jacking off Federson Mobile's

third-shift stiffs

for eight balls of ice in the alley

between Palentine and EZ's Auto Pawn.

Ronnie can't stop smoking pot.

P.B. Bremer

Todd says he likes to suck

six straight Falstaff's from a tall red glass

until he's too drunk to light his cigarette.

But tonight, the bail bondsman of their need's release

has closed shop, slipped

with tied tongue and stitched lips

into the empty spaces

hanging from no hope's dark star.

In the silence of night's sour hours,

heads pressed into plastic pillows,

their clammy hands

clutching stiff white sheets,

they pray for unknown gods

to cut a swath

wide enough to lead them out of uncertainty,

for fear to do what needs done.

Calendars

Slow-footed, shoeless, numb
we paced the antiseptic corridors
of the head house.
We swallowed our pills and waited
for reason to wind his wheel,
for Icarus to mend his wing, for the Tin Man
to hold his heart in his hand.

And afterward, when the doctor
buttoned us up in our new skins
rubbed raw and clean
on the electric bed of science, our progress
duly noted, we were discharged
from the therapeutic rooms
of our curious hotel.

Stuffed into the silver linings
of our lunatic smiles, we stumbled
into the bright white light of the world:

P.B. Bremer

landlords, dead loves, ex-wives
bad credit, no credit, contracts, court orders
car loans, home loans, alimony, child support
bankruptcies, bruised youth.

Home now,
showered, dressed, and medicated,
necessity pounding
in the hesitant bloodwork of our bodies,
we straightened our faces
and cracked the door,
the tentacles of those hideous squid
waiting patiently as calendars to kill us all.

The Bumble House

The Bumble House

In the Bumble House
we stumble
across the empty spaces
between the stars

between the comets
between the supernovas
between the black holes
and the hot rocks.

We wear its weight
its flex, its flux.
We shake our fists,
we curse our luck.

P.B. Bremer

Stranded

Sycamores sway

like battered sponges

in the breeze. Today

there are no hunters,

no shooters

shooting from the empty beach.

Today, only this—

a man, an anatomy of driftwood

stranded in the sand.

Three Stains of Winter

    I.

Dusk
trembles leaves

calls
rooks to roost

as shadows
grow against the ground

and the moon
fat and white

slips its fingers
down between the clouds.

    II.

A burl of winter wind
freezes the mind

like a shaft of accusation
strangled in the hand.

P.B. Bremer

    III.

Naked, blurred
beaten

winter's pensioners
rise

to serve
their fateful places—

the job, the classroom
the bar next to the car wash.

Soul sick, the heart
a quartz stone

one pink blind eye
blinking into the darkness.

Memoir

The raped, the robbed, the segregated

heart is a rage (or shame) love

will never water. Nights bristle.

The guard shack star

burns on the yard, on the nameless graves

lined swamp feet first

across the lip of the convict ditch

beyond the big house wall. Memoir

snake steady in its blood skin, pride

its mottled history's oily coil.

P.B. Bremer

Muddy Waters

When I leave this town
I'll go by train

first-class
on a rainy day

my head
full of Muddy Waters

my pockets
full of money.

Blue Note

Favor a sky
gray as a brain,

rain
        falling

like Coltrane,

hours that drift
without paddles,

question marks
stranded

on the flat, blank page
of the day.

P.B. Bremer

Self-Pity

lick your wound's wine,

bury heart's harm

in its baptism of scars.

Let your tongue's excuse

crawl cataleptic

into its dark confusion.

Poultice the carbuncle

of your complaint with gasoline,

light a match in the black

and burn, burn, burn.

Circus

Let the clavichord

play its steely notes

across the suicide's throat.

Let shadows grow monsters,

let monsters

bare their teeth.

Let elephants don hats

leopards silk shoes

pandas cravats. Dance

to the shattering of glass.

Tell only lies, steal

more than bread.

Honor nothing. Silence!

Here come the clowns.

P.B. Bremer

Lonely Ones

Let's hitchhike the empty spaces
between the stars.
When the galaxy's wild rumpus ends
and the asteroid explodes
we'll laugh the universe
back into its groove, hop a comet
bound for NOW, and we'll dance,
we'll fucking dance.

Deep Water

Swim beyond
the breakers

beyond
the ceaseless tide's
indifference

Tread the deep water

arms
raised above your head

your heart
shaking two fists

clutching angry stones

Separate Corners

The Basement of Unfinished Sentences

Behind each love's certainty

a doubt calls it home

to the basement

of unfinished sentences.

When love puts its clothes back on

to say goodbye

a man feeds on the stove ash

of his delusion, swallows

the savage abortion of its meaning,

stitches the last scar

across his flesh-starved heart,

and patiently waits to love no more.

P.B. Bremer

Conjunctions

Some Monday, as daybreak
rains from lawn to lawn
and school children
sleep steadily in their beds
and laborers hunch together for one last smoke
listen to the lovers across the block
fucking at their open window,
listen to pleasure's corporeal and metronomic
slap, lust's rough and honest message.
Let them wound and wound again
the dark and lonely spaces of their hearts,
nudity their chosen clothes.
And when desire's hurricane has passed
and the wind is but a whisper
and their garments lie scattered on the floor
and the two lie spent and broken on the springs,
be a witness, unashamed
and close the door
on this staid and private matter.

Marriage

After the argument, two bodies
burn, that house a harm,
two rings absurd.

Love's bruise
bleeds on/beneath/between
a separated silence.

This sham soon ended.

P.B. Bremer

Reconciliation

Let them begin again,
with starry constellations
tossed about their heads
like a cabaret of fancy hats.

Let them begin again
the long walk home,
no snakes for tongues,
no bees between.

Tattoos

Our marriage grows

away from us

into the musty trunk

of its bed

whose sheets are never ruffled,

into that cave

whose walls welcome us

to the great mistake

of its hideous tattoos.

P.B. Bremer

Between Sheets

We stood together, snow
falling through the street light's
bright white arc.

But even love's steady hand
couldn't lighten winter's weight
hanging from the knuckles of the sycamores

or the silence
slipping between us
like our guilt between sheets.

Tough Skins

8mm Man

Listen to his size 10
Converse high tops
slap Route B as he runs
between silent
black and white splices
of his 8mm memory,
down black top, over boils
of bubbling tar
broken open, netless hoop
above the barn
nailed useless above its patch
of gravel and grass.
Motorboats across the bay
don't know the child's cry
in her Christmas crib
or the boy in his chaps
with cap gun and Stetson.
Fathers waterski away from their wives
standing dazed on infidelity's shore
in Carol Brent knit mixers
and white canvas flats,
beating bread crumbs
from the dried soil
of cheating sheets.

P.B. Bremer

The Final Bite

When a thousand miles
from the final bite
our ugly love
collapsed in the Floridian tide,
I chucked our 10-karat marriage
into the waves,
curled into a fist the churl
made of us, and slept the night
with two wide eyes
that would not weep.
I swam freely the serpentine length
of your memory's flooded tunnel
in just one breath,
met myself beneath the trees
and watched me wave away
the hatred of your face
now nothing and no more.

Tough Skins

Tough Skins

Behind These Bars

I miss the freedom
of trees

my people,
what was home.

Familiars now are strangers,
now I sleep alone—
one bad animal in bed,

nightmare
without a name.

P.B. Bremer

Even Now

the green fields burn
on the red-hot rim of sunset.

Buzzards pick at roadkill
lying silent
on the bubbling blacktop of summer '76:

possums baring razors, raccoons
flattened in their tracks,
rotting dogs, a cat or two.

The evening's shadows
grow nine-inch nails
from every bale and fence post,
every branch and swallow

tilting their heads toward Hallsville

Tough Skins

where Grandma's plate of chicken,

her corn and gravy waits

for family to gather around her table.

Talk will rise and fall

and murmur on from open windows

as Uncle Daryl snaps and shuffles the deck

hand after hand

ignoring the night, the fireflies'

neon throb, a dozen cousins

scrambling, screaming, barefoot in the grass,

the delicate rumble of thunder,

the twin moons of high beams driving past,

heading home, stabbing black.

P.B. Bremer

January 8, 1965

The day I was born
I didn't know Carey Grant
and Leslie Caron
were a hit: *Father Goose*
for a buck at the Broadway Drive-in
or that day kids
would eat toasted cheese sandwiches,
a lettuce wedge and apple sauce
at the laboratory school
or that Elvis was thirty
and a decade from dead. Elvis!
who didn't know me,
P.B. Bremer, 8 lb. boy
born to George and Judith Bremer,
two proud and foolish parents
who never loved again
the freedom of their inconsistencies,
who never loved again.

Recollections of Mother

Mother, you made me
before I made myself.

I made myself unmade
and in my making came undone

falling ten stories to the street.

P.B. Bremer

Toughskins

A gap-toothed little country boy
wearing Toughskins and blue canvas Keds
argues with his mother.

She slaps him. He runs,
blind, furious
into the breathless, black
July night.

He swears never to return.

But when his fire dies,
when shelter's cruel necessity
has whipped his false pride numb,

he turns back, back to her
whose worry stains his window,

to her

who sweats her inquisition's
disappointed preparations.

Tough Skins

After Recess

When the teacher blew his whistle,
we froze.

Everyone but Curtis Crenshaw, the boy
who one day bathed his face
in acid
before burning his grandparent's
house to the ground.

Brady Johnson pressed his face
against the fence
where Mr. Quinn stood white and gleaming.

The Stotelmyer twins
floated perfectly balanced
on the seesaw.

Lisa Anderson
sat beside her shadow
on a bench.

The clock in its cage
above the double doors
that pointed us back to class
swept away a minute

P.B. Bremer

before the bell rang
and we filed inside
to practice writing cursive.

We wrote our letters
and read our books
and added up the numbers
on the board all afternoon.

We waited for the bus
to drive us home to have a snack
and hug our mothers.

Routine was the weather that we slept by.

Curtis Crenshaw?
He got dragged away for always talking.

Tough Skins

Mac

Where are you now
my dead bloody boy?

Are your bones
growing weeds
at the end of the fence

where the vines
still strangle
the trunk of the tree
memory burns on the bank

the day that Daddy shot you?

Duty's cold comfort
for a quiet man's sin—

country justice:

one dead dog
for one black calf

chased down
and killed
under the cobalt moon of midnight.

P.B. Bremer

Hostile Territory

Iowa, its winters
those icy gray whales
fevering our bad brains

until we snapped at shadows,
snarling dogs baring teeth,
or slept, one leg twitching,
whimpering in pens.

We went loony in our rooms,
paced the hallways of our separate silences,
ate quietly our bowls of glass.

How slowly spring's blue and heavy head
thawed that furious season's
sludge and dirty drifts,
rains that did not stop,
floods that nearly drowned us.

Tough Skins

Summer boiled the farmer's neck red.

When September demanded its Indian reprieve
we searched each morning for surrender,
the autumn frost its flag, so when fall
erected its harvest border,
insisting we speak its name with leaves,

we stared through its branches,
we ate the stars, the moon a perfect circle,
we breathed the midnight air,

a cool cloth, our fever breaking—
home in hostile territory.

P.B. Bremer

Sister Suzie's Head Got Sick One Day

In the snapshots
you wear your red and yellow
alphabet frock
and brown-bobbed China hair,
still five, caramel,
leaning into the *Berenstain's Family Vacation*
with a determination
barricaded against failure
or squat against the garage
of a lime ranch
stranded at the dead end of September '71.
The Indian has shed his tears
over Earth Day, over Hallsville,
over every wish we had not wished
in those blood-bath reds of summer.
Beautiful Buddha, though 40 years
mumble their ugly numbers
and memory is a catastrophe in trade,
let me build for you now
a bridge to cross, a tower to climb,
a city to save
with your glass heart.
Pawn youth's disappointed preparations
for a main sail keeling homeward,
your quaking mind a continent
trembling no more.

Backcountry

His favorite aunt is dead, the one
whose Missouri table twang
made the pronunciation of pie
as warm and black as the coffee served
in her cream and sugar cups on Sundays.

Two sons, a murder and a suicide
arrive to lift from the grieving city of her bones
memory's forgotten backcountry.

But her gate is chained,
her forty acres fallow.
The blackberry blooms no more.

P.B. Bremer

The Boy in the Box

He's an imp and an angel, a dreamer
a tease. An explorer of meadows
and a climber of trees.
—Hallmark card, 1965

On his second Christmas
he was given a train, a horse
a backhoe and boots

but miles of memory
swallowed dog and brother both—

Rabbit run, rabbit run
rabbit run before the madman comes.

Pull a pistol on reason.
Pull it on fact.

Those skeleton keys are easy
when its smoking barrel
marks his way to the grave.

Blue Billy

You were the latchkey kid, the boy
who skated barefoot on the corner,
trailer trash who lived on peanut butter
and potato bread, pinball, KISS spitting "Black Diamond"
from the turntable spinning at your open window.
You were the kid whose sister slept around,
whose mother and father drove home late
to drink themselves dull from fifths of gin
behind closed curtains, the one
that the block moms refused to let their children
toss the ball to. I was the farm chuck from Mizzou
who refused to tuck his shirt into his trousers,
whose jowl pulled punches from suburban boys,
their fists fat as apples going for the throat.
We were the dirty seeds that climbed bridge trestles
drunk on Grain Belt, rats who stole bikes,
black hearts that girls frowned or smiled at
in the dry and airless ways of virgins.
Where are you now Blue Billy?
Eating your lunch in a Tenderloin kitchen?

P.B. Bremer

Thumbing across South Dakota
on your way to Wall Drug? Maybe your drunk
in jail cell in Spokane
or dealers have shot you and left you for dead.
Thirty years later your denim face fades
in the December five o'clock dark. Now I bend my back
over memories too cold to color.
Our summer's over. You have followed the dead
into the empty spaces between the stars.
I am no longer troubled by those cankers
that grew their thorns ahead of us, those years
that we could not see from where we stood
smoking reefer under the ball park's weeping trees.
Having pedaled behind your shadow
as ugly as our years were crooked
and gotten nowhere, I quit you. Cheap years
spend like pennies, and I must be to work by nine.

Juvenile Detention, Marion 1981

The shark
swam
within us all

as our eyes
flashed
along white walls

ten feet
taller
than ourselves,

white walls
ten feet
taller than ourselves

outside
our empty windows
on a Saturday.

P.B. Bremer

YMCA

After sleeping three nights
in the back seat
of a '67 Beetle
abandoned at the dead-end
of Prospect Avenue,
after four days
yanking out the entrails
of an old stone Tudor
with a crowbar
for three bucks an hour
and a hoagie every noon,
I rented a room
on the 3rd floor
of the Hagerstown YMCA.
For two years
I screw electrical sockets
into their blue plastic boxes,
run Romex room to room.
Each night
I trudge across
the Pleasant Valley putting greens
to bag groceries
at the Parkview IGA
before I backtrack
those circular seas of green,
climb three flights
to room 302,
and smoke my last cigarette.

Vitriol

That young summer, I threaded
10' sticks of 3" rigid pipe
coupler to coupler
up the catwalk at Alcoa Gravel and Sand
with a monkey wrench
burning in my hands, Leonard Black
screaming "Faster, faster!"
day after day
until I dragged my ragged ass back to the Y,
showered in a three-man stall
and blew a $10 wad of 1s
night after blessed night
drinking dollar Tequila Sunrises at Leo's Tap
to rise blistered in the 4 AM dark
to lug my toolbox through the rain,
spitting vitriol, a Lucky Strike
pinned between my teeth.

P.B. Bremer

July, 1986

Jane Miller slapped me in the face
with a hot, flat Miller Light. The air
swelled with embarrassment. It stank
of our recklessness. Days later
I stole a bottle of 12-year-old
Irish malt whiskey from my father
that went down so smoothly
I climbed into Janey G's lap
and wept between her breasts. Angry men
looking for work between boarded storefronts
stalked 1st Avenue end to end
while debt-sick farmers shot themselves in barns.
When the dope dried up
the dealers moved on to Davenport or Moline
and lovers, anonymous as deck chairs,
sweated in their beds.
Cedar Rapids lay dead-eyed
in desperation's black bunk.
We celebrated its uselessness

Tough Skins

with weenies and beans.
When summer solstice bled crimson
over tall crops bearing yellow cobs
skittish on their stalks,
we ran naked through the traffic
of our bodies. But when the air
grew big-bellied and the sky gray green,
dawn unplugged its constipated chamber
of rain, washing the skrim from our impatience.
We lifted our heads
and with dry tongues and split lips
praised mercy's weary wind between us.
Our wives and mothers shopped the off-brand racks
at the going-out-of-business sales
and we were proud of our new shoes,
our neighborhoods loud with porches
gossiping on their blocks,
each man's heart an open boxcar
flashing on its track, each eye's hope
chuffing down its silver rails toward August.

Calling the Body Home

Opening Act

When I was young, my clothes were new,

my feet stepped flat and sure on straighter legs.

I clung to trees, I raged in rain,

I was proud and mad and unafraid.

But the days, they hide now, one behind the other,

stare back to an opening act too good for truth

wet and white and green, stare back

through regret's cracked glass, kaleidoscopic, cruel.

I think I'll blind my eyes with arrows,

I think I'll bleed like shot dogs do.

Yes, when I was young, my clothes were new,

my feet stepped flat on straighter legs.

But now I blind my eyes with arrows.

Now I bleed like shot dogs do.

P.B. Bremer

Dead Man Walking

I knew, while reading Camus
between two tombstones
in the Unitarian graveyard,
that behind each love's certainty
a doubt calls it home
to the basement of unfinished sentences

that at the dead end of days
a single street lamp
will burn away the empty spaces
between the stars, no ambulance
to save me, no arsonist
to torch black years best forgotten.

Death? I'd run naked
through the traffic of its body.

Memory's foghat sweated and swelled:

Tough Skins

Blue Billy leaning into summer night's
hot with hashish, his face
bright as an arc weld,
a Lucky Strike pinned between his teeth.

Black Cats, bloody carcasses, roses drawn
across a pallet of green, Blue Bird #9
speeding like a plump yellow amphetamine
grinding gravel down RR-33,
a barn full of rain.

Life *was* a B movie
crowded with a credit of extras.
I was the modest cop, man with cigarette,
bozo on the bus (#6), the shirtless boy
with no nose.

Years passed each other on their runways
and though I earned new shoes
and paid my rent on time, faded faces
still send me postcards inked in scabs
or rain checks wet with someone else's letters.

P.B. Bremer

Thistle

Why must I go on now,
a grown man
buckled up with worry?

I'm tired of cutting thistle,
sprinting from stir to stir
stanching flames—

solitudes fevered cogitations,
the brainwork of dead loves.

Drown regret's good intention
all candle lick and spider.

Swallow its corpse stone,
parlor the blind eye.

Denial bellows its own stone hearth.

Empty Wallet

Where does a man turn
when every street
has changed its name?
How does he clear the weeds
choking out the sunlight
without a scythe
and two arms to swing it?
When the job is gone
and all the women have
locked the doors to their hearts
and his wallet of options
is empty
and every meal tastes
like the barrel of the pistol
he's unholstered, what plea
will make its way to a god
he no longer believes?
When the pianist plays silence
and the poet has burned his work,
loneliness builds him a jail cell
where he waits patiently
for the spiders to arrive.

P.B. Bremer

Two Men Pissing

me and the man beside,

two broke-dick horses
taking ten minutes
when it used to take two.

Different days
different places
different doctors
indifferent to all but eyes

we strain to read
C from O
at the end of the Stellen chart

seeing clearly
our caving faces,
two sagging trailer parks of scars,

waiting for our wives
or the world
to slit our throats.

After the Prostatectomy

Five slices of the knife
bruise blue,

the black walnut
of my sex

yanked
bagged and bloody

through my navel.

Stitch after stitch
dissolve

like iodine in water
seed skin in oil
rust in cola:

the colander of time.

P.B. Bremer

Nausea

When the bottom bucket of your gut is

gurgling and black gas is

shooting out your ass and you

spit gizzards of bile

on the rug without thinking,

the slit of your attention

narrows to death's fine white point

and you think to yourself

today is the first, the last

blank and nameless check I'll ever write.

After Sixty

It's pitiful how
puny one shrinks
after sixty.
The butt
riding lower and lower
over grass blade legs
beginning to
second guess
each step, the mind
softening
into a quiet anxiety,
eyes cataract,
back bent.
The dangling hands of chance
can't touch the toes
nor the mirror
make of its hairless stranger
a chum
on the way to the grave,
the heart
forced to listen
to the muffled trouble
of love
through a thimble.

Dying's bland bite
is a hard home to swallow.

P.B. Bremer

Cremated Remains

Even with the door closed and the window shut

you can stand pissing in the wind, the day

so dry, so lonesome

you climb into bed with your clothes on,

sleep twenty minutes at a time

between slurping flat water from the tap

and the post-hole shovel

tied to your mind's typewriter

strikes granite all afternoon,

the cracked gasket of your heart

leaking the suicide brother

buried in the box in the basement.

There's no map for that,

no legend to measure the miles

back to the birth of his breathing.

Eulogy

When our bedroom windows
bloomed
pink, green, and gold

before emptiness
emptied their color

and we woke
screaming
from the silent movie
of sleep,

our balding, august bodies
aching, flatulent, fat

we stood
uneasy
on our feet, waiting
without words,

P.B. Bremer

lost in the airless closet
of our thoughts.

Our shoes didn't fit,
our salamander hands
couldn't tie them.

Tomorrow
was the language
we did not speak,

only *years ago*—

orphan memories
seeking their casket's
compensation.

No Quarter

No fever
sweats
for no blood
boils
behind the temples
of the dead.

Theirs
is an exit
of salt, a thirst
troubling living's
dark harvest,

the thresher
leaning haughtily
on the handle of his scythe,
the grave jack
on his shovel.

P.B. Bremer

Here the Furnace, Here the Fire

Lay the body
across the cold stone floor

brow closing over
the monochromatic

slow motion movie
that is mind

guilt the grist to grind,
sin its salutation

the fine film
from which the blood pumps.

Wake, now or never.
Here the furnace, here the fire.

The Moment Knows

In summer, around six
114th Street dreams of sumac
burning so bright in my eyes
I want to die on the ocean tide of the highway.

I stand on my back deck
and stare into aspens chittering.
I shiver, listening, without words
to the wind chime.

My mind's not right.
The poisoned sludge of its blood
gropes toward a funeral:

Mother dead five years now, her ashes
bagged in can of decaf
rusting on a freezer.

P.B. Bremer

Lance Griswold's bones

bleach in a fern grove

under a Sequoia in the Cascades,

my brother buried in a box

labeled CREMATED REMAINS

while a thousand miles and forty years over the fence

my dog's carcass rots beneath a cornrow.

Only the moment knows

these seeds

which grow inside each second

where the world sleeps

to the lodestar of its heart

and I slip twilight's last pale star in my pocket.

Dead Ringer

I shuffle between students,
cemetery stones
without names.

I grow cold,
reason
rotten to the root.

I watch a spider
drop, dangling
from its invisible wire

and die
on the waiting plain
of my desk

like time's crawl
down the works
to a stopped clock:

night

        to twilight

day

        to dawn

then nothing.

P.B. Bremer

The Branch

He lay
broken on the couch,

watching
from the window

fog
hang its wet

and heavy head
between the trees

when
without rhyme
or unreason

Jim Harrison
walked across the bog,

Tough Skins

dead seven years,
winding his way

up Antelope Butte,
his name taken

spoken in crow.

The man rose,
smiled

pacing
the empty moon rooms

of his heart.

He turned on the radio,
listened

to the tilt of the rain,
name

P.B. Bremer

and no name,

name

and then none

in the belly of his own bird

singing silence

from the branch

that does not bend

or surrender.

Forest Prayers

Let me die

in the forest of my wife.

Let my hands

that held no son

no daughter

shake neither bat

nor brick

regretting nothing

but the broken gourds

of living

in the dim-lit

cathedral

of God's one good eye.

P.B. Bremer

Calling the Body Home

When the August sun sets
calling my body
into the hoard of locusts
beyond the road
leading home no more,

before my shadow follows it
one slow foot
then the other,
mute as the universe
that refuses its congregation of stars
their shine,

hold my head in your hands,
kiss me from this fence
you cannot cross
and give me back my bullet.

I'll mend these broken spokes
then burn them.
I'm a long-line skinner baby,
I won't be passing here again.

Acknowledgments

Though no poems previously published appear here, I would like to take this opportunity to thank Al Markowitz, editor at *Blue Collar Review*, for the man and his magazine were the first to give my poems a public platform from which to speak, the first to take me seriously as a poet and a writer. Without Al's trust, I would have surely given up long ago and gone quietly about the business of teaching.

About the Author

P.B. Bremer was raised in the corn and bean fields of Missouri and Iowa. He was educated at Mount Mercy University, the University of Iowa, and the University of Denver respectively, where he majored in English, English Education, and Professional Creative Writing. For the past twenty years, he has lived and worked in Denver, Colorado where he teaches English full-time in the Concurrent Enrollment Program at Front Range Community College in the School of Writing and Literature.

P.B. Bremer

Tough Skins

www.ingramcontent.com/pod-product-compliance
Lightning Source LLC
Chambersburg PA
CBHW020946090426
42736CB00010B/1288